MW01206262

THE ASMAUL HUSNA

THE 99 NAMES

OF

ALLAH

WONDROUS NATURE

COLOURING BOOK
VOLUME 3

SHAMEEMA DHARSEY

1ˢᵗ Edition March 2019

First published in March 2019
by Shameema and Mukhtar Dharsey
Cape Town, South Africa

Introduction, back cover copy, and colourist by M.C. D'arcy
Art Direction by Mukhtar Dharsey

I give thanks to the Almighty for all the blessings bestowed upon me.
Thank you to my parents and brothers for all their love and support.

For more art and illustration go to:

www.shameema.co.za

© Shameema Dharsey 2019 . All designs, illustrations, typography and patterns in
"The Asmaul Husna, The 99 Names of Allah, Wondrous Nature, Colouring Book Volume 3"
are copyrighted by Shameema Dharsey.

This book is made specifically for, and only, colouring in.
It is for personal use only, you are not permitted to sell anything using these designs.
All rights reserved. Not for commercial use. No part of this book may be reproduced or used
in any other unauthorised manner without the express written permission of the author.

The 99 names of Allah: The Asmaul Husna

The human mind cannot conceive nor understand the true nature and dimensions of Allah. This is stated in the Quran, Surah Shura; 42:11:

'There is nothing at all in the universe; nothing in all existence- that is the misl (equal/similar) or even the likeness of Allah.'

Soon after the death of Prophet Muhammad (Peace be upon him), scholars searched the Quran and the Hadith (sayings of the prophet) for words that would describe the power and majesty of Allah.

The collection of 99 attributes accorded the Almighty in the Asmaul Husna by collators and scholars go some way for the average human mind to ponder over and understand the indescribable attributes and majesty of Allah.

The Asmaul Husna is often recited in a melodious lilting manner that reaches deep into the psyche. The mellow chant instils a deep yearning to be close to the Almighty. It is often recited in thikrs (prayers), stirring spiritual inertia into action.

Humans are blessed with colour vision to see the wonderful things in creation: the blue sky and the seven colours of the rainbow, the green fields and forests, and the myriad colours of flowers in bloom. We have ears and hearing to savour sweet sounds, and then there is touch-sensation to carve and fashion beautiful objects. All human beings have talents.
In expressing art there is no right way or wrong. Everything that you deem beautiful is art. Art is soul-food. It is medicine for loneliness and often used in troubled times to heal the soul and mend broken hearts. This colouring book, primarily for adults, is another step to reach out to those who have a yearning to combine innate artistic talents with the spiritual.

So, splash a million colours across the pages with joy; it can be profound, yet fun and fulfilling.

- M.Cassiem D'arcy

INDEX

ALLAH

BISMILLAH

1. AL-JALIL

2. AL-KARIM

3. AR-RAQIB

4. AL-MUJIB

5. AL-WASI'

6. AS-HAKIM

7. AL-WADUD

8. AL-MAJÌD

9. AL-BA`ITH

10. ASH- SHAHID

11. AL-HAQQ

12. AL-WAKIL

13. AL-QAWI

14. AL-MATIN

15. AL-WÀLI

16. AL-HAMID

17. AL-MUHSI

18. AL-MUBDI

19. AL-MU'ID

20. AL-MUHYI

Allah

Bismillah-ir-Rahman-ir-Rahim (In the name of God, the Most Gracious, the Most Merciful)

Al-Jalil (The Mighty)

AL-KARIM (THE GENEROUS)

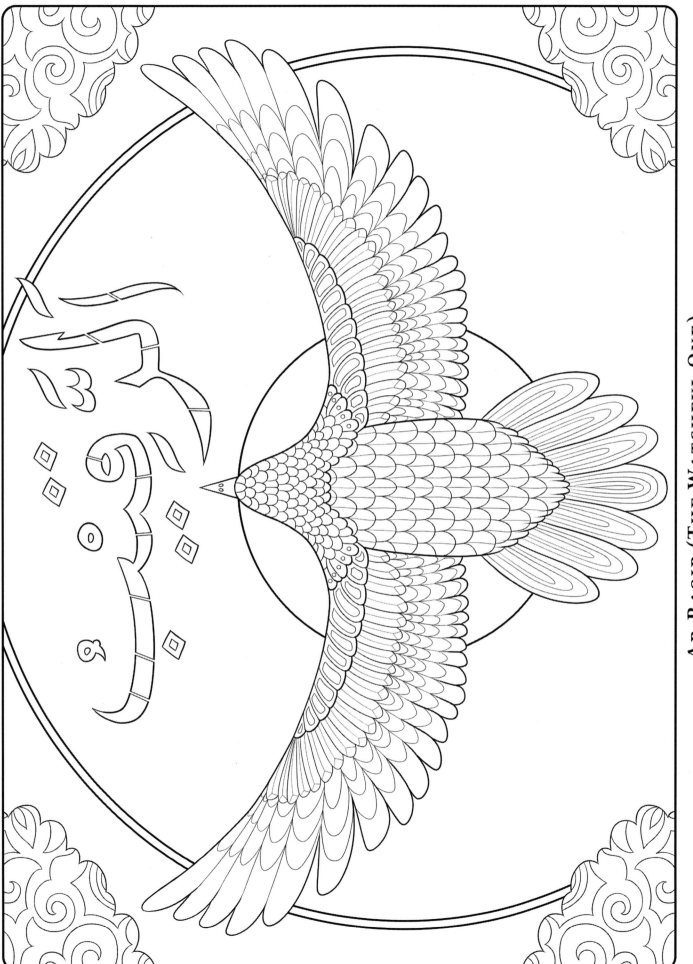

Ar-Raqib (The Watchful One)

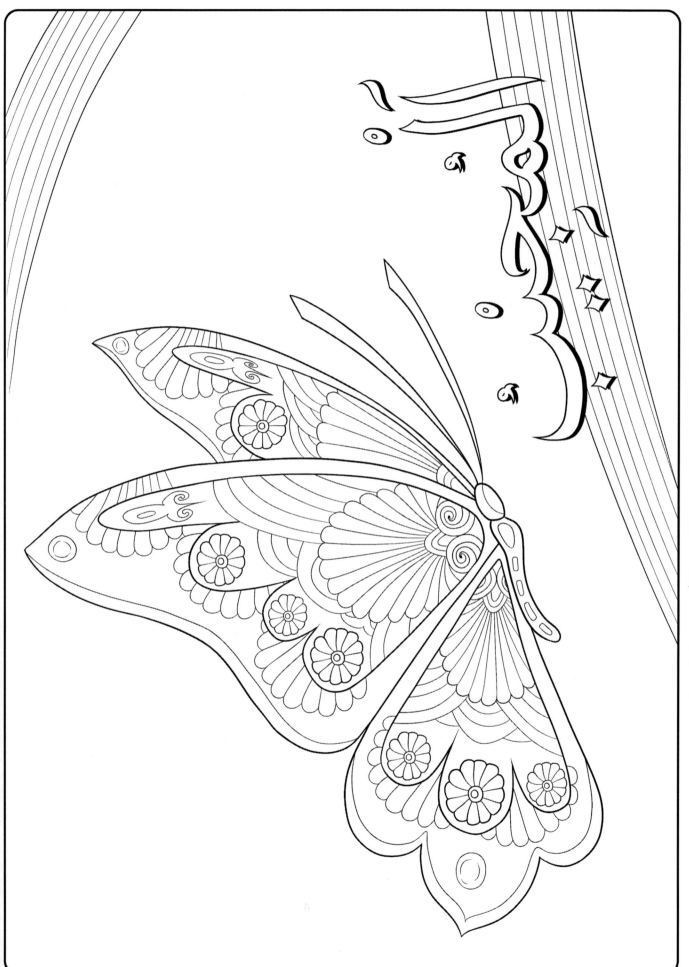

AL-MUJIB (THE RESPONDER TO PRAYER)

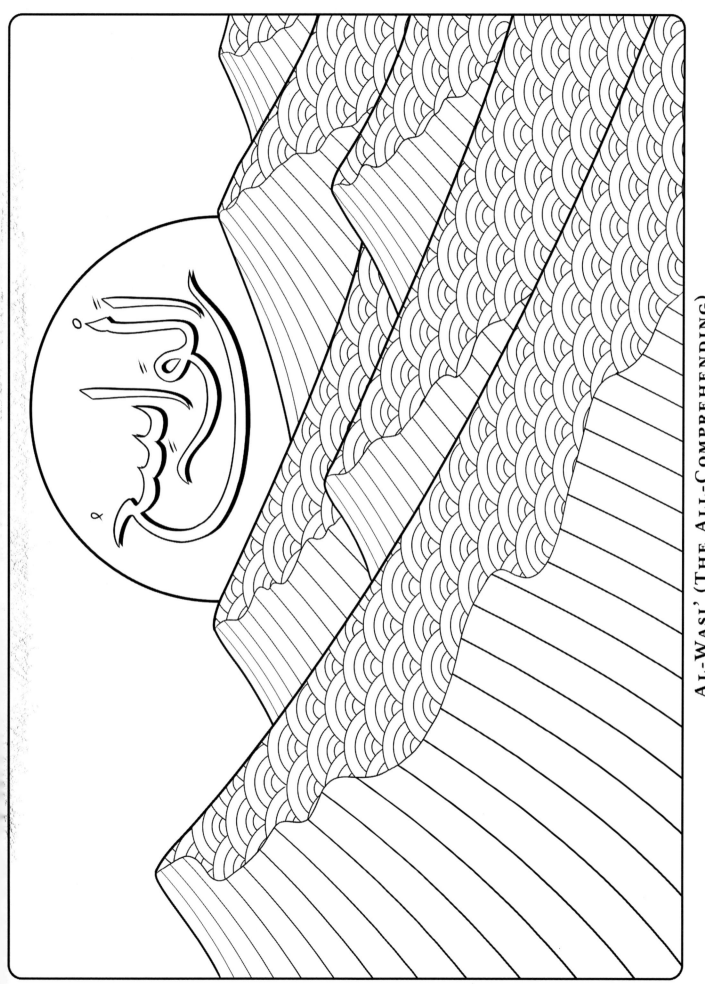

AL-WASI' (THE ALL-COMPREHENDING)

Al-Hakim (The Perfectly Wise)

Al-Wadud (The Loving One)

Al-Majīd (The Majestic One)

Al-Bàith (The Resurrector)

ٱلشَّهِيدُ

Ash-Shahid (The Witness)

الْحَقُّ

Al-Haqq (The Truth)

AL-WAKIL (THE TRUSTEE)

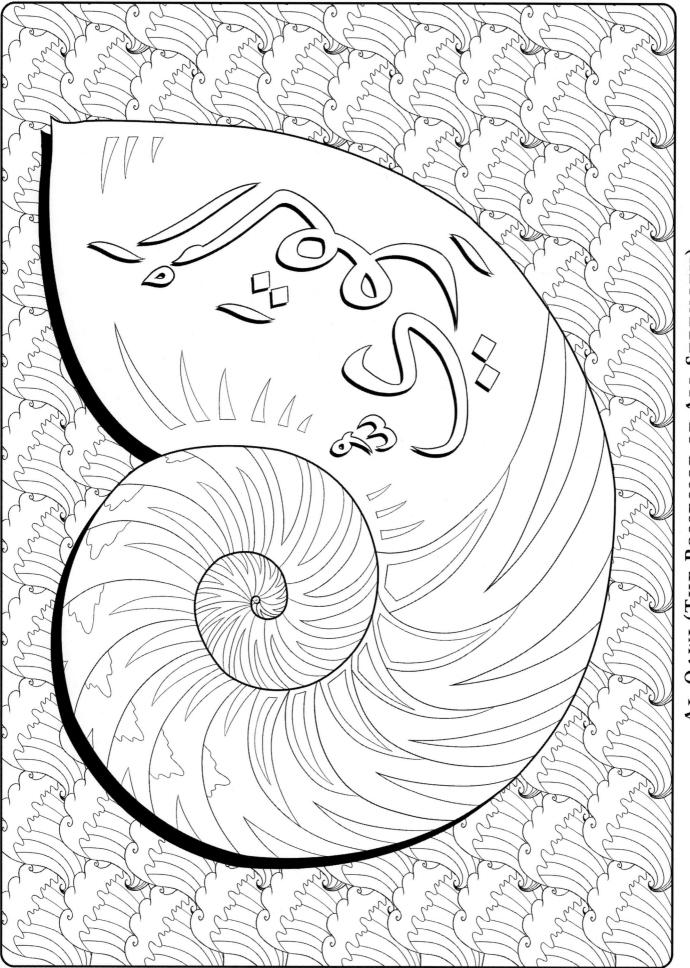

Al-Qawi (The Possessor of All Strength)

Al-Matin (The Forceful One)

Al-Wāli (The Governor)

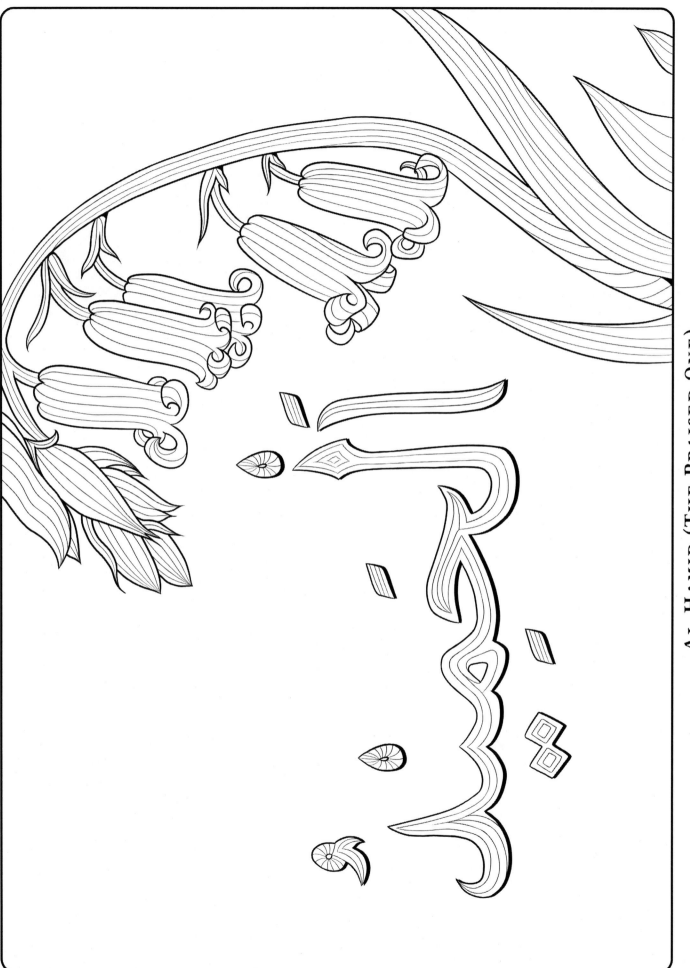

AL-HAMID (THE PRAISED ONE)

AL-MUHSI (THE APPRAISER)

AL-MUBDI (THE ORIGINATOR)

AL-MU'ID (THE RESTORER)

AL-MUHYI (THE GIVER OF LIFE)

Made in United States
North Haven, CT
25 June 2025

70129454R00030